CHRISTMAS

SATB and piano or organ

And can this newborn mystery

Alan Bullard

MUSIC DEPARTMENT

OXFORD
UNIVERSITY PRESS

And can this newborn mystery

Brian Wren (b. 1936)

ALAN BULLARD

Duration: 4 mins

This carol is based on the hymn-tune 'High Leigh', written by the composer for the above words.
This carol is scored for small orchestra (2fl, ob, 2cl, bsn, 2hn, timp(opt), str). Orchestral material is available on hire.

Printed in Great Britain

OXFORD UNIVERSITY PRESS, MUSIC DEPARTMENT, GREAT CLARENDON STREET, OXFORD OX2 6DP

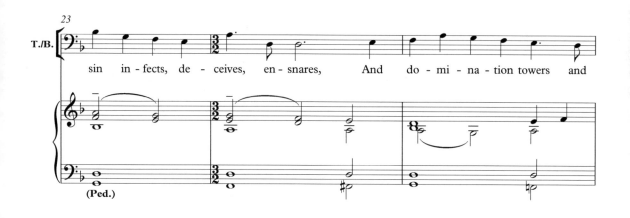

sin in-fects, de - ceives, en-snares, And do - mi - na - tion towers and

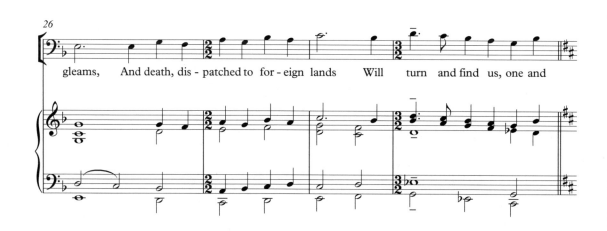

gleams, And death, dis - patched to for - eign lands Will turn and find us, one and

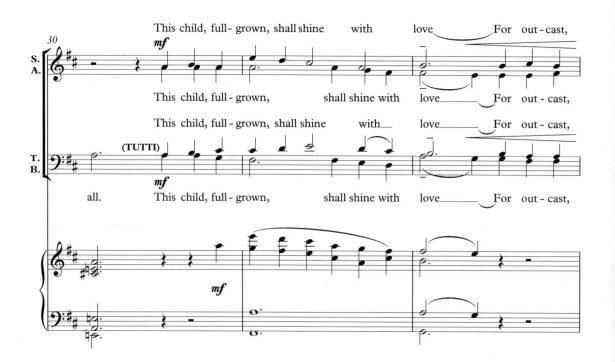

This child, full-grown, shall shine with love_____ For out-cast,

This child, full-grown, shall shine with love_____ For out-cast,

This child, full-grown, shall shine with__ love_____ For out-cast,

all. This child, full-grown, shall shine with love_____ For out-cast,

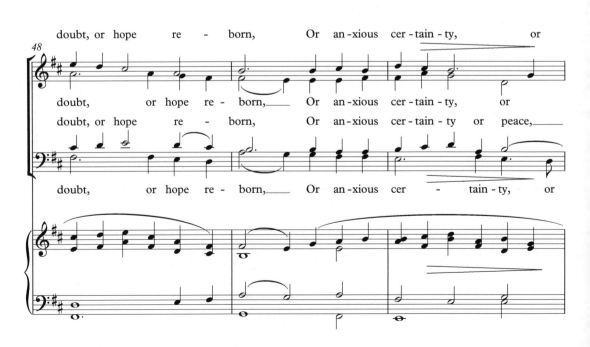

(**Piano**: omit upper small notes)
(**Organ**: omit lower small notes)

peace, We wor - ship, trust, and rise to
We wor - ship, trust, and rise to
peace, We wor - ship, trust, and rise to

serve An in - fant learn - ing how to

feed.

November–December 2008

OXFORD CAROLS

Oxford publishes a vast array of Christmas music to suit every occasion and choir. There are pieces and collections for services, concerts, and carol-singing; pieces for SATB, upper-voice, and unison choirs; *a cappella* carols and carols with piano or organ accompaniment; and a wealth of traditional favourites alongside new carols by leading composers. There are also over 250 orchestrations of carols from *Carols for Choirs* and other collections available for hire, including versions for brass, strings, and full orchestra. With hundreds of individual titles and an impressive range of carol anthologies, Oxford provides a rich collection of the very best in Christmas music.

Selected carol anthologies from Oxford University Press

Carols for Choirs 1–5

The Oxford Book of Flexible Carols

For Him all Stars, 15 carols for upper voices

A Merry Little Christmas, 12 popular classics for choirs

An American Christmas, 16 carols and carol arrangements from North America

An Edwardian Carol Book, 12 carols for mixed voices

Alan Bullard Carols, 10 carols for mixed voices

Bob Chilcott Carols 1, 9 carols for mixed voices

Bob Chilcott Carols 2, 10 carol arrangements for mixed voices

John Gardner Carols, 11 carols for mixed voices

John Rutter Carols, 10 carols for mixed voices

Mack Wilberg Carols, 8 carol arrangements for mixed voices

Sir David Willcocks: A Celebration in Carols, 18 carols for mixed voices

World Carols for Choirs, SATB and upper-voice editions

Christmas Spirituals for Choirs

The Ivy and the Holly, 14 contemporary carols

OXFORD
UNIVERSITY PRESS

www.oup.com

ISBN 978-0-19-336637-4

9 780193 366374